AIR-PROOF
GREEN

AIR-PROOF GREEN

Maleea Acker

PEDLAR PRESS | *St John's*

COPYRIGHT © 2013 Maleea Acker

ALL RIGHTS RESERVED. No part of this book may be reproduced or transmitted in any form or by any means whatsoever without written permission from the publisher, except by a reviewer, who may quote brief passages in a review. For information, write Pedlar Press at 113 Bond Street, St John's NL A1C 1T6 Canada.

ACKNOWLEDGEMENTS
The publisher wishes to thank the Canada Council for the Arts and the Ontario Arts Council for their generous support of our publishing program.

LIBRARY AND ARCHIVES CANADA
CATALOGUING IN PUBLICATION

Acker, Maleea, 1975-, author
    Air-proof green / Maleea Acker.

Poems.
ISBN 978-1-897141-57-1 (pbk.)

    I. Title.

PS8601.C535R43 2013   C811'.6   C2013-903177-4

COVER PHOTOS
front: Joan Simon, "Burg, Pallars Sobirà"
back: Maleea Acker, "The Floating Fields"
DESIGN Zab Design & Typography, Toronto
TYPEFACE Montrachet, Fountain Type Foundry

PRINTED IN CANADA

Contents

To the Unstated Theme

MINOR 15

TREE FROGS 16

THE SIERRA CABRERA ECLOGUES

    I. TO THE UNSTATED THEME EACH VARIATION COMES 18

    II. THE JACKAL BIRD 19

    III. NIGHTS IN ALMERÍA 20

    IV. CALLE ALCUDIA 21

HEART AT VALPARAÍSO 22

THE ALMOND IN THE EARTH 23

Farrera, Catalunya

DRAMATIS PERSONAE 29

THE AQUARIUM 31

SPRING SNOW 33

WALKING TO L'ESTANY 34

FIELDS OF BÁDIA 37

CUCKOO 38

A SLANT VIEW 39

THE COMPLETED OBJECT 40

STUDY IN BLURRED CONTOUR 41

EQUINOX 42

TALALA LLEONE (LLEONE HILL) 43

PIXEL 44

HUERTAS DE MARÇAL 45

The Inheritors

THE INHERITORS 49

IN THE FIELD 52

WAITING FOR A SIGN 53

MAISIE THE DOG 54

SALAMANDER 55

MARINA MARIGO WIND 56

METIER 57

WORK 58

CINQUEFOIL: THE BLUE, BLUE DAY 59

THE SPRING CREEK STORY 60

SHOTPOUCH 61

GEORGIAN BAY 62

Little Windows

BLUE 67

BLUE MOUNTAIN LAKE ELEGY

   I. TWO DEER 68

   II. VERMILION 69

   III. SLIP 70

   IV. ADRIFT 71

   V. ALMOND 72

WALTZ 73

RED 74

THE BOATHOUSE 75

BELL CLOCHE 76

RIVER HOMES THE CABIN 77

MOVING PICTURES, SILENT FILMS 78

ACKNOWLEDGEMENTS 82

AIR-PROOF GREEN

To the Unstated Theme

MINOR

There is no
> rhythm to
>> its passing; it is not a

cadence to set one's clock by but one's breath.
> How deep is our yearning tonight?

Engines tack history to landscape,
> a spiral stitch. First
>> the call

begins as cacophonous voices
> in the coulees and riven ravines,

gathers as one chord, throws itself
against stone, gives arch to valley's arc, seals
metal to earth in a parabola of sound.
> The river of wheels follows. Spectral

flood water
over rock.
Not engine but
magnetic.

> Backdraft of the passing,

the leave-behinds: dishes,
> our small arguments,
>> sleepless hands sorting night from warmed sheets—

a final song. So faint,
a window must be open.
> Epilogue.
>> After
>>> happily ever
>>>> after.

TREE FROGS

Outside is singing.
                Beginning in
awkward twosome, the
syncopation all
                    wrong, then they get it together and rise
and fall from perfect to trios
to perfect to
pocket combs
        berry husks
                rye seed jumping open at a touch.

     I'm as thin as the skin
that connects my dog's belly with her thigh.
She's dreaming beside me.
                In her mind green stretches for miles,
the lily pad corridor opens into light
ironed smooth and live.
            She trails the boat.
                  She's a hollow reed that smiles.

      When I was nine
I counted minutes with friends until my birth time.
4:08 pm. The embroidered chair, the skylight
of my mother's room, the step
      I fell from and lost
a tooth on, the drop into depth—
     then this long casting back
to the single number,
               the thing gone.

      In Catalunya
Lleone Hill grows verdant.
      The bells move to summer pasture and the stream's twisting, twisting,
          it pulls away
from everything, frogs in its head rush,
can't be touched without affection,
      doesn't glitter under birch and cliffs but takes
their colour and bends it
        until blue
    snaps free from green: swallows,
            sea, blue so blue it's shaking in its sleep.

THE SIERRA CABRERA ECLOGUES

...it is

all things lustered
by the steady thoughtlessness
of human use.

— ROBERT HASS

i. To the unstated theme each variation comes

Mountains begin in being's far plains;
    all day it continues to be anything else.

Secateur clips of the olive, black branch rainfall
    on the sharded earth. Whistling man

who calls for his dogs, dogs' nail click on road,
    road sigh, road hiss into dust,

dirt's joy when dinner's bowl is scraped clean.
    There is no language being cannot become,

no animal its pumice does not survey.
    In its terraced dictionary, all unsaid thought,

understood by the grass and the humming sun.
    Spread wide at night, miasma and pollen,

jackrabbit who knows when to freeze
    and again be the field.

ii. The jackal bird

      Between each roar
of the jackal bird
      the world unfurls,
each call
      a word, each
word followed by the unbraiding
      of air,
glissando.
      The jackal bird knows
it rends, knows
      how necessary—
it takes its job seriously,
      at dawn, at half-moon,
floating at height
      with its little griffin scream,
its plump tail,
      its snout damp and cool.
Hearing its cry
      a burst of fear, then heaviness,
stillness, a strange
      gilded lift of breath
that could be played—
      a bench and piano,
rain in summer,
      a morning, a feeling
of great formality.

iii. Nights in Almería

Sometimes
after the valley of the oranges, having
seen the bees in wait, knowing
all sleep now in the house, having not upset
the thin bowl of water which is this night spreading way

you can see
the matter thrown from afar,
stand gazing at its silver splendour in warm air, the whirlpool it pulls
into being. Everything still.

You can't pluck it from air
but each thought turns numinous braille.
Darkness hovers, befalls the groves,
and something speaks too swiftly to be understood.

Listening, you don't know—
is it the machine starting again?

iv. Calle Alcudia

after Inger Christensen

Yes, Inger,
happiness is a kind of fear.
I am crouching
in dried winter flowers at the side of the road
that leads me home.
It is not my home, but we must—
now I have kneeled, and something
crunches under me, while dusk scatters
and the last year's grasses wave
and the horses in the orchard below breathe
and in my head Reich's breath while the Pulses release.
I am terrified, Inger. The dusk comes
unconditionally.
        Oranges glow, as they should,
radio antennas scrawl against the sky
as it unribbons from pale to Majorelle blue.
There is no respite, but *flash*, the arpeggio of the chord, and *flash*,
two pale dogs step from twilight to lean against my legs.
We are a trifle
lit in front of the sky,
think just of this leaning.
I am green, stiff-kneed.
A faint warmth from sun-side walls
drifts through me, like entering
then leaving
an unwalled room.

HEART AT VALPARAÍSO

It is happiest pretending
to be a wren. In a rain-filled stone pool,
the hundred thousand things and the little cross

of its legs as it leaps and kneels at wash.
When the gardener moves to orange tree
it flies to clothesline; as he trims the figs,

it returns to leaf of water.
Drives its neck into the pool,
crosses its legs and twirls, dives again,

shivers the beads along throat
and breast. Stands. Almond of its voice,
milky, pebbled song.

THE ALMOND IN THE EARTH

Mojácar Viejo is a semi-terraced, pyramid-shaped hill of bronze-age ruins in Almería, Spain. At the top is the vestige of a water cistern built of stone and plaster, carved out of the mountain's peak.

for Hephzibah Rendle-Short

If memory could augment shape. If still water
could smooth stones. The almond in the earth shines—
pocket in rubble, flat-topped beacon, pan of air,
twisting—a mouthful an airy pause.

(Long sluice of stones lets water enter, water-coursed pathway,
aqueduct of intention, the lip worn round, the drop now gone.)

But if rock were supple.
Piedra—a word in any language. It's speaking
from a kind of storminess. It rocks on its edge.

Turned inside out by thirst, the height a sensibility;
highest curve, exclamation—
where past once pooled in a peak.
The creation of cistern illumined

fragment, sentence, rock,
pottery shard, plastered seam. Its top
air, the seam an arc of compass.
It lies at 54 degrees.

(And across the opening, your two strings mark
deepest point, where water

reached its hunch. At the crossing, your two stones, whipped and wound:
tug of tension, midpoint
of mountain, thought and query,
iris and egg.)

It's whole. It's thought, but
open to sky. It's always been here.

Farrera, Catalunya

Slate, wind, chough's black wing—

trying to force this
        I can only be drawn in.

DRAMATIS PERSONAE

FARRERA - village of forty residents, Spanish Pyrenees
TALALA LLEONE - hill opposite Farrera
THE AQUARIUM - valley between Talala Lleone and Farrera
PORT DE MONTANYA - mountain pass between Spain and Andorra
L'ESTANY - high altitude lake near Port de Montanya
ST. EULALIA - church between Farrera and Burg
L'ESTUDI - slate house where visitors to Farrera are hosted
CISCU - washing machine repair man (Barcelona), gardener, historian (Farrera)
CESCA - cook, storyteller
OPPEN - shepherd, photographer
ANNA - Oppen's wife, shepherd, rose-oil maker
LALA - friend in the village
LLUÍS - Cesca's husband, expedition leader
BURG - village south of Farrera
CUCKOO - *Cuculus canorus*, heard frequently, seldom seen
MARÇAL - patriarch of Farrera, singer, deceased two years
JOSEP - autodidact
MORTUELO OWL - winter resident owl
CARBONERA COMÚN - Great tit, winter resident passerine
SWALLOWS - *Hirundo rustica*, migratory

The action takes place over two months, in Farrera and surroundings within walking distance.

THE AQUARIUM

Because the village girds the edge of the ridge, a greening ribbon tints the bottom and the other peaks enclose us in rock, in swallows and sway.

It's here I've really wanted to fly.

Measuring up, or measuring out over the quarter mile, finding there is nothing the swallows haven't already invented in scrawling glide and suicide curve around the balconies. You're my minnows, I say, and you've said it all.

It started as a waterfall. The highest floating fields tipped when a mountain shifted. As if the glass they were held in listed. Some of the poplars fell. Others developed kinks and continued to grow.

The water far above me is higher every morning.

Someone sprinkled a white road along the bottom, near the anemones, the submergible and the golden snails.

What there isn't: dust, fire, loneliness.

Sometimes the swallows break the surface. Then a whirlpool develops and the cuckoo's tone jumps, weather is sucked in and something like thunder follows their wing beats down a trail of glossy surfaces.

What there is: breath, drop-spins, envy.

Still, the way some old women—thinking to be a part of things—toss feathers for their nest-building.

Once the *Guardia Civil* showed up in tanks, which flooded when they opened the tops, and we had to harness the dogs to pull them out.

Some nights I think I'm gliding like them but it only lasts until the piece is done.

The blue-feathered ones are my favourites. As I've felt more at home I've begun to believe it's where I got my eyes.

SPRING SNOW

Winter returns to Farrera
as argument, new air—
and as amnesia. Nubs of tender-grey stones,
and birds: how they turn peculiar.

Mountains cloud,
abate—the world
brings out its tin boxes
to collect the colour, hide it.

Snow lasts longest
by the humped stream's back,
below the ficklest fields, among cherries,
poplars and mud.

Birch-red,
tufted unsaids, Sweet William
ice-bled leaves and the grey
feathers of swifts who tilt past
the village no matter their mood.

The wind drops; it begins.

WALKING TO L'ESTANY

*

Just a minute.
Ciscu, Cesca, Oppen, Anna, Lala and Lluís.
The mists rising from Barranc Mallolis, we walk through a break in the rain,
up from Farrera to the high fields of Pic de l'Estany.
To Roc del Cúcut, St. Eulalia, meadows of Badia, of Valenti, of Paiola, of Burg.
A swift flips over itself, its wing rings the stones. Swifts fly cleanest at dusk,
at dawn. By Sant Roc and Llosera, snow stiff in the distance,
I'm still as can be.

*

Stories Ciscu carries, stem by stem.
Roses de la parada, meadows de la Caterine, Susanna, Generosa, el Marçal,
the woods cremat. The streams are running. We walk up,
up and up in shirtsleeves. Gate of the mountains, Mata de Burg, Rocs Rois,
the floating streams, a rise. So, mangled, nested, thinking, we rise,
a prickle hedge, a plume. *Just a minute,*
Ciscu pockets a stone from the river of Sort's banks.

*

Song of *Carbonera Común*:

Listen closer, he says.

*

Before we walk, he teaches grafting with twine, sun flagrant.
Look closer. He fits the wild rose stock with the burlesque graft, *maybe
this won't work*, blackbird's clipped cry unmatched to its size.
Swallows cleft each row of trees. One by one
by one, by names. Then we are walking, it is colder, my head afire.
Ciruella in the pastures, almendras don't grow here, nor higueras, limons.

*

We emerge into upper meadows. Blue pools on the slope, slate huts
in the folds. Walls hidden, pastures hollowed, shorn like the pelt of a sheep.
I am still. Port de Montanya, Casa Marçal, Casa Josep, meadows of Burg.
Wild walnut ruins, coiled sisal, roof timber fallen,
birdhouse nail in mortar, in mortar. When the bloom begins
each field swells to pool, as bracken, birch, poplar, rose clamber.
Ciscu linking the world through voice: a scythe
made two patterns in grain, left-light right-dark half-moons, the numinous
cut in the stalks. So, coo becomes rou coo, as red pine
gives way to black. So, we climb.

*

Just a minute. I carry the huertas of Ciscu. In his gardens,
as the thumbs of two cuttings slid true, he pointed skyward, *buitres*,
vultures thrumming, a fan-tailed storm of sky. To learn home
through scent. Inner palm—wild mushroom; back of hand—dried meat; beard—
smoke sweet pitch of pine amber shining; elbow—the gleaming bath,
his house's one finished room.

*

We're lakeside, in snow, spring vanished. *And this tree*, he says,
only in Rocs del Ribal. Sola de Garata, Borda de Baro,
Masia de Burg. *Look closer*. L'Estany a blue reflecting pool.
L'Estany, walking, the wind from Pic de Stat,
the skin not strong, we sink through lake surface, we sing, snow hollow
an approximation, a transparency of blue.

*

The sweetest are walnuts from Burg. Small lungs doubled,
boned, delicate. After grafting, we wrapped the cuttings in twine, poured wax
and pitch to seal. I brought tea. In the house dust heaved through lit air.
I took a picture. Alpine swifts like minnows scrawled
the dragon-scaled roofs. *Just a minute*, he gave me a fragment of resin,
coal-singed, glowing—*this one's from where we'll be*.

*

CUCO COMÚN *Cuculus canorus* (Cuckoo). *Más oido que visto, con su familiar cú-cuu
que se oye a gran distancia. Vuele sin levantar las alas sobre el plano del cuerpo.*

*

So the splice of intimacy.
The rafters of space hung like theatre, *just a minute*, the house
that unfolds like a flower, *maybe this won't work*, the cupped stigma,
the slate and sandstone star. Bordes de Burg, its huts for summer sleeping,
Corriol de Burg, where the bells go in summer,
Huertas de Ciscu, where he touches and binds, L'Estany de Burg,
where what's born begins to sing.

FIELDS OF BÁDIA

Slipping off ridges into delicacy and impermanence,
the fields have a lily pad sway. A high floating shimmer
    laid out in layers, turned ice, receded—
where swallows give intelligence its curve.

    Snow can't muzzle
the tensile plain and the scythe
is summer's river on its fluid pelt. A scree,
    fields flicker, they creep with the weight of a sea.

At centre, they unfasten. Basins of artless paragraph,
    clear answers, forthright gaze. Here
things come to their losses
and can laugh. Pouring from mountain

without mountain's reserve,
chestnuts anchor their edges and hooves fold them
    until they chatter loose at night.

    If green were serous
and in its unhinged pour,
    akin-to-joy overflowed.

CUCKOO

Dusk, again. To stand
at the stone house's window,
stare down the valley's stage. At the impetus

of a season—nothing speaks
clearly but the indeterminate beginning of trees.
A low hum before the first bars,

an old tapestry
washed to burnished thread;
I didn't know brown could have such depths.

But it's attention I'm failing at,
and the birch with their pumpkin tassels
show this, the clay poplars

in their floating fields,
pressing key by key
an unknown song—

drift of beech on the ridge—
one strand at a time.
There is no such thing as a thing unworthy.

Fine and thick twigs, cracks
in the world. Hear *coo coo, coo coo*, urgent, hilarious,
a study, a success of unmeasured form.

A SLANT VIEW

It delivers to us, as much as us to, a space in which meaning is suspended.
— MAURICE MERLEAU-PONTY

A slant view is better
than full disclosure.
Half the poplar hints
as it means to be thought.
The margins of the wood
draw us the way
the midst does not. It snows
but the rounded pastures
free themselves as snow falls.

Beside this valley, another,
less beautiful, and another,
narrower. The birches
skid the slope like cranes.
Folded thickets drain into pastures, tilt
gently like the jade sea.

When attention does not find itself
wanting to know,
to complete, *the world abandons it
(and the viewer) to idleness.*
Never the whole, only

    part, a trunk slipped free of frame
    and curtain; a branch
    indistinct in spring, glassed thought.
    For an hour, single things illumined:
    paintbrush, exclamation,
    gold leafless drift in the leafless
    brown grove.

THE COMPLETED OBJECT

The completed object is translucent, being shot through from all sides by an infinite number of present scrutinies which intersect its depths and leave nothing hidden.
— MAURICE MERLEAU-PONTY

    Nothing with name
can be completely unveiled.
Ciscu and I in the orchard. The simple nouns
of apple and rose, the approaching thundercloud
of translation.
          Nimbus blue like St. Eulalia's walls,
colour rising in reconstruction like a flood.

Behind the kitchen in his one room
wood and stone house lies the double marriage bed
separated by white curtain with red poppies. There's an accord
    in what passes from his lips
in earth, his rows of trees, the flamboyant cherry,
three varieties of quince grafted to the stock.
He says, *All the year's wait*
for so little fruit.
        In the orchard—
meaning floats away down the greening slopes.

    I'm savage too in another language,
untethered, charmed only by beauty or Latinate name.
As I also mine the philosophers
for their loveliest words—*resonance, wonder,*
he'll be as I understand him, he'll be
very little in the end.

STUDY IN BLURRED CONTOUR

Mute adulation
brimming in the gulley,
      rising from underground streams.

It doesn't have a far side but a constant interior.
Deer on what appear to be
      the vertical terrace of its ribs.
Marçal rasping their call from his balcony.

Why this place? To be seen and
      not know the question.

Birches pull trick handkerchiefs from wood.
White road of snow, streams
drawing anemone and bird.
      The acclamation's heart is based

in the ridge where shape
      steadies to cherry and stone.
Two hundred feet or so below the red pine grove.

Somehow at the centre are small, clear caves of bracken—
What to say? How do they go?

EQUINOX

Snow makes dog's fur of the groves.
    Night falls even with day—no benefits, no
deliberate harm, and the snow devil that rises in wind
    dances like a character of indeterminate morals;
if he finds her, she may suffer or be happy the rest of her days.
    So, my sullen relation to landscape: in sun,
working art into a frozen ground I am happy,
    leap down the hill. At dusk, all the failures.
We never see ideas or freedom face to face.
    It's not long enough, and even when at its longest,
won't be long enough. Wild hellebore, sage, sticks
    for the chough's nest: all buried. Wait all day
for *the world is calm*, only to see dusk
    slump onto the horses' back, sung down
by *pit chit pit chit pit chit*. This blue snow
    is tungsten—malleable negative
that fits the skin like musk, that snakes in
    like stars, oceanic,
the cold colder each call.

TALALA LLEONE (LLEONE HILL)

It's the real deal. For forest the ultimate contour.

It undulates at night. It's the great aunt, the aerial inquiry,
the ball of wool unspinning itself back to fragrant fleece.

It may be my childhood.

Animal, when it gives that small shake before returning to the graze. Mineral,
in flecks of mica pliant as clay. Unnoticed

small arpeggio of the bass line, backdrop, distant scene
painted by the apprentice. The lovingly drawn last letter
that says nothing, everything.

But how it contains, leans into its own tufted life.
To go up to something. To attach oneself like a burr. To go up to something
and remain forty days. Its rib cage nudging mine.

It contains and does not harm the heart of the question.

It asks what I think I'm asking. It suspects it was not wrong.
?? it says to me.

The water between us like glass. If I put my hand out,
wood daphne, thin streams and the honey blossom smell of new alder,

its lanterns hanging flames in the air.
??? it says. I laugh I put out my hand.

PIXEL

Flying in snow and sun after the storm,
joy in my mouth like a peppered bird.
I am heading up the mountain
to place squares of coloured canvas on the white
pixeled beauty of the slope; the painter wants
to know her work from afar. Except I have moved
from protected village—smart villagers—to the windward side,
where sleds and skiers congregate for powder,
most procession-heavy beat of squall.
And the squares fling from my grip, swirl like petals up the slope—
the painter, with camera at the balcony, signalling with her red sweater—
I'm chasing pure colour up the mountain,
and the blue sky smacks down on me
like a palm, while the stick trees draw one another.
I'm faster than the snowboarders, who must trudge;
I weigh nothing, I am free;
nothing touches me but cool sun.
I catch and pin them with snowtacks, circle, watch for the signal.
The stick trees lean in.
I'm made of nothing in this picture—
square of sand, square of sea, squares of sky aligned,
and a girl facing sunward,
no reason no proof
no outcome known.

HUERTAS DE MARÇAL

Anna, the bells are sounding and the light
is light, rather than just what we see.
How can I feel at home?
These are your bells, Anna, and the *Mortuelo* owl is sounding,
the mountains clear, the nightingales returned. It's so blue,
the church window liquid, the door of my house red, and those far horses
your neighbours, your sheep just back from the fields.
I see something just now that plucks me.
Ciscu's pine sap, coals and smoke
like amber, like liquid that rises to the touch.
I've inserted the cutting, Anna,
into the wild rose's stem. *Quitaba las espinas*,
tied it with sisal, spooned the wax. The sky is too large
for this, what, this wing? A matchstick swallow
strikes itself. The sun goes. Josep leaves, Ciscu will leave.
I am falling into your leas, Anna.
Tan earth pelts the slate cliffs of Burg. Something's
trying to take off but can't endure the weight.
Wild cherry knotted into quince, the cutting
now higher than its stock.
He's smiling at me. *Goliara*, record player bird,
playing, Anna, your walking songs,
we could remake the world like this,
these tiny insertions of air-proof green.

The Inheritors

THE INHERITORS

I am travelling through the mountains
on my way to ask for money from the inheritors.
Descendants of those who dug up the earth, enfolded men in mines
and broke our unions. It is warm,
a little cloudy. I am barefoot in the old car. One after another
the workers' towns, named as a try at belonging,
who thought to stop, with a tag, the old world's
bad bread and bricks through windows—here
      is the new land, where names mean nothing,
everything. Shifts of mountains frame the highway,
not growing but slowly wearing down. One shale shard
skids off the sloped abutment, sinking
to a nest of leaf just forged,
old carrot lacing out of the ground.
          A comfortable heat
nudges the car window. A new diplomat, I rehearse
for the Boards and their coffers, veiled in the distance.
            Long were we searching, through years
of black milk, until arrival in a city
where a woman crowned, holding fire in her fist
proclaimed us free. From Vilnius also sailed
the ancestors of Jonathan, who imagined more gold
in the name Buenos Aires; his sailed south, ours
stayed north. A century later, we chanced to meet
there—his apartment of one window, his wife and child
slipping food from the kitchen, while the Spanish
words for the body curtained around us.
            The Bow Valley gives way
to the last climb before sinking
into the plain. The air yellows. Soon,
the first housing development.

      My grandfather was fired
six months from his pension, from the Los Angeles missile factory,
the machines' beats shaking the floors
as he walked in for the last time, then stuttered
to a late career in movies, making sets, hammering
trees to the imaginary lakeshore, while the stars
                rode by on their horses.
At eleven, my father was screen tested;
in photographs, flawless, a welling optimist—
my grandmother would not let him go.
To be a star was to misuse the names,
to forget who has not enough. But who does
                not know the pleasure
of arriving in a new city, the language
unknown and every corner exchange,
every call tossed down from a tenement
so secret and glory-filled. Dust stretches
                in a brown haze
as I clear the foothills and fly
into the opulent plains. Lens clouds appear
on the horizon; the storm season is about to begin.
I do not know if I cannot remember
or never knew the names of my great uncles,
      the ones who stayed in Russia,
and married, and fathered children, and then
were overtaken by a cloud of ash.
                At the airport, everyone is friendly.
I clear security. I wait in the pod
that the United States has made in this country,
and practice asking for a little more.
I picture a sphere, floating. I imagine
                we are rising up,
and west, as the plane will.

I imagine we do not know when
we will land, or what fortune we will find,
in what language it will be shouted or
spoken, or what each name will mean.

IN THE FIELD

The river belongs to someone new every hour. I am safe
in the meadow's cloth like an unopened envelope. A robin

searches for its lost locket, head up, tries
to remember, head down, he looks again. Some bushes

have forgotten winter, and hoist their five fingered flags of green.
My heart is a colt with Pegasus in its blood—

my hooves don't touch the field. I send coded messages
to my friend and when she writes back

the sun is real. Grasses bend to the left, to the right—
they don't know which party to support! On the other side

of the mountains, tyranny ends and everyone
has enough. A spider succeeds in attaching to my pen, which leans

like the tower of Pisa. A thousand foreigners watch as
he completes his circus routine of loops and silks, ties

my shadow to a pine. The strand stretches in the sun—
we recline and admire his work.

WAITING FOR A SIGN

Spring comes to the mountains.
    Every third breath of wind
warms the nape, then
    every one.

I take a footpath I think will end in the valley.
    It stops at the cliff face. Maybe this
is where I was supposed to go?

Someone below laughs.
    Thermals, but no hawks.
        I wait near the edge.
    My heart runs back and forth like a gate left unlatched.
Soon, it is down in the meadow.
    Heartless, I step to the cliff
and hover in the heat and newly hatched poplar leaves:
lemon-paper, toothpicks. A crow,
    or maybe raven,
ladders the air to check me out.
    Circles once.
    Refrains from comment.

MAISIE THE DOG

Desire is a robin's egg in her mouth, undamaged.
Attentive as water drops to their larger selves. Empty,

but consumed by bees, leaves, voice, her clattering bowl.
Mid leap, she is love's fulcrum, lake's plum

unbroken before her. A believer in
the anxiety of pleasure, pressing toward the mark.

Lake's shine mottles the trees, the world's
greater meaning flicks a feather,

adjusts its cape, snaps its fingers for her—
kindred, lusting, black eye, pure ear.

SALAMANDER

Tumbles from my fingers to my cuff
and burrows. Emerald lumined eye, jelly paws,
bark body and tiger belly bright. His tail a blade
of thick sedge. Each ponderous, stop motion limb,
the crook'd elbow, the fan of the toes, the gentle flick
at conclusion of each watery step. Coolness,
the Mogami River. His head nudges
my wrist, no momentum,
the fourth beat rest in tetrameter. How long?
    The back foot lifts,
hovers, a boneless, incandescent home.
I set him on my knee.
I am a bad person, too curious, too eager to touch.
He turns his head to see, then away,
the little mechanism of his thought-calm unpacks itself
    as he leaps to brush,
becomes akin to leaf litter, stick or sunlit shaft.

MARINA MARIGO WIND

That it knows why halyards are made. That it lives
to make a boiling ribbon of the mast.

That it tenses spring line and aft in
endless combinations,

dreaming the hull through the arc
of its leash. Small bones of the tug;

ticker wheel of the release;
voiced only by its intimates—

sometimes, to know the world,
we must build something,

must be in the way. Because of us,
the beautiful doors opening inch by inch.

METIER

Let that one morning all displacement ships away.
A wavering left—vestige of forest, sweet plain
where water was. Every city crack distinct as foreign
script, the mind collects but does not alter, combusts
into crowds, alleys to the interior plaza,
an inappellable expression
of startle. White pages mobile like winter swans—
can I say it? I love this more than anything,
anyone: to watch, a failure,
                    as the beautiful, uncaught line swings
in wide circles around the dusk-lit crane.

As below, the smaller oaks, their brown sails filling,
drift the meadow like old men, this bench, that,
wherever the pretty ones pass them by.

WORK

Sometimes you can fly this thing. You hover
above the furrows and stare into the warren
where bracken stores winter during spring storms.
It dips like a swift at the slightest touch.
Lets the cat off. Lets it back on. Your task
is to notice everything, relaxation the best method.
Forget, look down, there's the raven. Forget,
look up, thirty vultures, fly specks in the sky.
Something more important is always
happening where you're not,
                    the way it should be.

CINQUEFOIL: THE BLUE, BLUE DAY

She walks as if to meet him on the road. Wears the winter coat
knowing it is enough for the shadows and too much for the sun.
Forest creeps in on all sides like a semaphore. In mind, the music
of body, areola, inner thigh, mouth. Four years only the beginning
of being alone. The dirt road, packed and pathed with gravel.
Robin, stream rush, the occasional logging truck with thin sticks
from the mountain above the cabin. A track of sun in early spring,
three miles while the salmonberry climbs the ridge.

What she cannot see is the US mail driver sitting in his cruiser,
empty bags at his side, his beard red as rosehips.
That the creek will rise to roadside and brandish dogs
and apple borers and skunk cabbage flags. That the small, swaybacked
horse who takes grass from her hand at mile two
will permit a small touch for each bundle presented.
Her hands bleed from the blades. The mare gives one glance, then returns
to the shade of the planted pines, her foal lying in sun studying
his own hooves in the mud. Sometimes a rift in life
cannot be turned into poetry; it sits in sun
and takes and takes and takes the light until birds burst from it
and the river muscles past the crumpling willow
and the steady, thoughtless chewing and smoothing goes on,
showing the curve of his eyes
as they once closed in pleasure in the morning,
showing the walking stick, showing the horse's
pleased and painless thought.

THE SPRING CREEK STORY

Beginnings meet their endings, Katherine Hepburn's head
on the reporter's shoulder as they traverse the poolside walk, singing,
"Hello C. Dexter Haven!" Full throat spring when sun comes,
chrome and capacious in afternoon dress. Here in Spring Creek,
when blackbirds come to investigate this small mess of coat and pen on the path,
bee joins, and with Rufous hummingbird, they sweep the ridge clean
for the music one cabin down. The voice a kind of water carrier,
a bowl slaking the bluff. He's stopped answering the phone,
and in this first extended silence, pain,
muted by alcohol and what else can be found, reaps in her
something like the true love always adjacent, never until now within.
It coats her like pollen; everyone can see the bright wash.
The oxalis burgeons ferociously, the root-tilled earth softens
for the hand that plunges in. We think things manageable
only when a slow-posted letter leaves hope for reply.

SHOTPOUCH

Odysseus tramps up the dusk hill, the blooming on all sides
as his mind lays down its same routine.
Song sparrow an occasional startle out of something bodied and musty,
as though having made love in the afternoon and then climbed
to the lookout without washing. Crouching to watch the sun
fold the world and there's the scent, not unpleasant,
but not like being alone. Or perhaps like being more alone than ever.
The firs wash to orange. He's pretty sure, in this version,
there's no Penelope to go back to. No wind in weeks and the rain
drops straight onto metal and woods with its one long one long
note of sorrow. Laughing at the idea of desire as anything that could quench
or be quelled. There's a bracken fern declaring at his feet.
He can't eat it, it's not a fiddlehead, though it has that same spiral of could-be-joy.
The oxalis makes him ill. And the dead mouse by the piano
made the wood floor look like obstinate hospitality.
He throws another rock over the cliff. Aeolus tosses it back,
along with the bleat of tree frogs, the shuffle of a forest finding its chair.
He shifts to unkink his legs, his heavy lidded eyes like oxen in their stalls
lowering themselves, kneeling on their fore knuckles,
letting the stiff boards and the soft manure sift between each hair.
Even when we know, he thinks, we usually have it wrong.

GEORGIAN BAY

Already, I have lost it.
Words fix things firm and the sun
pins beauty to the world.

But out where wave met ice cobble
the sine of water
lifted the drifts and dropped them—

a cloth slowly weaving itself
for a shoreline of bone china—
I climbed past onto a fathom of water

and rose, and fell before the unfrozen bay.
House, tree, book, star;
all slipped away. The aquamarine

ice of Georgian, like a swing,
a lover, a wing, solidity hinged.
For the certain answer,

for our successes, for completion,
this offering—a moving surface
the wave drawing near.

Little Windows

BLUE

Mayfly leaves, Octoberfly bursts forth.
White crepe ruffles, blue chicory body, translucent wings.

Take the rush and pull of raking,
the roll down the hill. Take sun's calming

sheen on the cheek, a girl in the grass, the book
thrown aside. Take the liquorice whip branches,

loons' arrival to the broken pond, prisms quick
as snow. Take the new stained glass,

the grey gardens, seaweed sheen of Brussels sprout leaf,
the black of a month without moon. Octoberfly, bloom

as pure falling, your Moroccan blue thorax,
your crinoline bustle, chaliced wings.

BLUE MOUNTAIN LAKE ELEGY

i. Two deer

Two deer race the water's edge, swing through
cold sun, close the circle
at the rain-filled river. The younger leaps for opposite shore—

*

There came a time like a dark wood.
I could see no shapes of trees or
name the plants below. Home along the winding road

I drank until I could not stand. TV on, sofa
as bed, I went down upon the boards, running
as though water, muted, labyrinthine.

Every hour a train
from your country. After midnight
no call, just wheels.

There is a bridge outside Copenhagen
that arcs and ladders over a sea,
then disappears into its centre

like a children's myth.
When the love that held us broke,
it fell to pieces small enough to take.

The taste and texture was gravel.
While I ate, a great bird stood over me
and struck me again and again with its wing.

ii. Vermilion

White-pine needles gone gold.
Winter settles steady as shoreline duff,
its great pulleys
              hoisting your world out of view.

*

A green wall
divides my life. Birds,

fishes, foliage—
things disappear.
I can no longer get through.

Sometimes, remembering
is a thirst; I go out on the lake—

when I dip my hand
the losses return.

iii. Slip

Broken stage where shore tips up,
the peeling root—rough warren, carbon heart—
the set beneath the woven scene.

*

At night in their stalls the boats nudge one another.
Water reads out its wavering scrolls. One by one

the house's lamps burn out. A thrush
hovers above the dock, its cry from one beam

then another. The lake multiplies,
timpani of the gunnels—

a kind of questioning.

iv. Adrift

To unlatch from pier to the auditorium
of water. To be glaciered, to take late sun,
to come at an angle.

*

Your shore is a museum of winter.
I scull past its sepia monuments. The sign says
the land of give and take.
Vermilion maples, a curled black bear,
a podium of ash.

The pines arrange to parcel air and turn it hollow—

the maps say *tired of not getting there!*

None
       chart the bottom.

v. Almond

To pass through pain
      merely be beside—
the deer springs from shore, rivers the air.

*

I lift the lake from its curve of stone.
The hard skinned bottom, the inner bone.
Above us, sky whirls. We glide through forest
as fall muffles the paths.
Pearl surface scratched, the spherical current
and indelible blue: it rests at breastbone, balanced.
In my hands silver water spins and spins
but never overflows,
cresting fingers, mercurial.
Behind, darkness,
perception's root and field.

WALTZ

In my dream we waltz about the Great Room—
precise compass adjustments, north to
southeast, south to northwest. A clear day
turned igneous, the screens thrumming,
lake calm in the centre, blown to brocade by shore. No fire, just
this wide wash of floor to draw into relation,
a spirograph. Eyes closed
I give up the lead.
Outside, the ridges of forest
slip against one another
like the painted set of a moving sea.

RED

At the intersection of three ridges
Cezanne's gift: the unblurred heart.

Midsummer's story so often told
the erotic bleeds into each leaf.

Not lithe but with carriage,
finally joy. I close my door

but the little window of my eye
shafts a light across the lake.

THE BOATHOUSE

    To have as ground this wandering floor.
Its speech inside out, unvowelled,
each slip sidling a craft.
    A star grown wild, humming waltzes,
reveries. Burning cool as phosphorus, the nails
nestled in their beds, the church-beamed ceiling making room,
alchemic lead lake now auric air.
    Underneath, it's ashore but leaping,
and water speaks in syllables, glottal stop
              glissando on woodblock. Set at angle
to predominant wave, the linkages,
the run-on sentence in love's most intimate voice.
    Eyelid of the lake,
its wing extended,
to leave is to burst into dream.

BELL CLOCHE

Inside the room we are skin to skin.
Love's breathing comes in
        through winter wren's
endless song, rain
sifting faultless down the glass.
    The storytellers put down their pens,
the fire dies as light rises. Immersed,
        we're ahistorical, we're akin.
Bell jar of the periphery, water
sheeting down, the leaves
      drawing up from the dark.

RIVER HOMES THE CABIN

Born of the thicket itself,
turning pages, settling the score, smoothing over river, river,
riven mind. Changing, it rests.
    Enough, enough, it haws. *There is a sorrow so old and silver
it's no longer sorry.* Tell it straight, it cajoles, without breath. Unroll and roll and roll it.
No one is the saviour they want to be.
    Come on, baby, let's dance.

    You let it in.
Uninvited guest, it glibs and murmurs and unravels
every plan, all the best laid lies. Little steamroller,
black-eyed boy who can't stop
speaking, his bright limbs flashing with trout—
        every word undoes your life.
Matchless, buttonless, inkless world you were born to,
      it won't, as it punches your sternum,
           kisses your face, freezes your feet,
              let you leave.

MOVING PICTURES, SILENT FILMS

Drive with one hand. Pull me in and smoke for us
as interior happiness tips and pulls history free
of the root-tangled body—

I wanted you first in a bookshop, no sound, no greeting.
I stepped close. My head slipped to your woollen chest,
perfect into the shoal between collarbone and rib—

Drive. I'm leaving
my wild mushrooms on the kitchen shelf, my forest's bloom
of red currant and rose, Bachelard's pool in the dirt by the firs.
Steer me through the manicured park—
what people who live in cities call a wood—
						I'll be still
in that river of your shoulder and my dark grief
trying too hard to be sweet, not bitter.
				But like Indian plum, it is both—

ACKNOWLEDGEMENTS

Thanks to the editors of the following anthologies and journals, where some of these poems first appeared: *FONCA: An Anthology of Canadian Poetry*; *Force Field: 77 Women Poets of BC*, *Poetry from Planet Earth*; *Rocksalt: an Anthology of Contemporary BC Poetry*; *Fiddlehead*; *Fowl Feathered Review*; *The Malahat Review*; *Other Poetry* (UK); *Prism International*.

My gratitude to the places where I wrote many of these poems and to the people who care for them: Blue Mountain Center in the Adirondacks; the Banff Centre; the Centre d'art i natura in Farrera, Catalunya; Fundación Valparaíso in Mojácar, Spain; and Shotpouch Cabin in Spring Creek, Oregon.

To Beth Follett for her continued dedication to publishing in this country.

To those astute and patient writers who helped coax (and otherwise) this book into final being: Tim Bowling, Beth Follett, Tim Lilburn, Drew Mildon, Alayna Munce and Karen Solie.

The subtitle of Section One of the book and Section One of the "Sierra Cabrera Eclogues" are lines by Wallace Stevens. Other poems also owe a debt of gratitude to his work.

"A Slant View" and "Equinox" contain lines from Maurice Merleau-Ponty's *Phenomenology of Perception*.

"Talala Lleone" owes a debt to Wittgenstein and Jan Zwicky.

Section Five of "Blue Mountain Lake Elegy" contains a line by John Ashbery.

"River Homes the Cabin" contains a line by Don McKay.

"Moving Pictures, Silent Films" is originally the title of a Great Lake Swimmers song.

VIVIENNE McMASTER

MALEEA ACKER is the author of a previous poetry collection, *The Reflecting Pool* (Pedlar, 2009) and a book of essays, *Gardens Aflame: Garry Oak Meadows of BC's South Coast* (New Star Books, 2012). Her poetry and journalism have appeared in journals and anthologies including *Force Field, Poetry from Planet Earth, Rocksalt, I Found It at the Movies* and *Best Canadian Poetry 2008*. She holds an MFA in Writing from the University of Victoria and lives on Vancouver island.